LIGHT IN THE NIGHT

Spirit Photography at The Cottage

LOIS ANNE SMITH

Copyright © 2014 Lois Anne Smith.

All photos in this book were taken by Lois Anne with an Olympus Stylus, 14 Megapixel Digital camera in the garden surrounding her home and The Cottage in Ellicott City, Maryland
Illustrations by Beth Ann Leitner

"Harry Edwards Healing Sanctuary, Shere, UK – www.harryedwardshealingsanctuary.org.uk"
Email Lois Anne: LoisAnneSmith@verizon.net
Visit The Cottage online: www.LoisAnneSmith.com

All rights reserved. No part of this book may be used or reproduced by any means, graphic, electronic, or mechanical, including photocopying, recording, taping or by any information storage retrieval system without the written permission of the publisher except in the case of brief quotations embodied in critical articles and reviews.

Balboa Press books may be ordered through booksellers or by contacting:

Balboa Press
A Division of Hay House
1663 Liberty Drive
Bloomington, IN 47403
www.balboapress.com
1 (877) 407-4847

Because of the dynamic nature of the Internet, any web addresses or links contained in this book may have changed since publication and may no longer be valid. The views expressed in this work are solely those of the author and do not necessarily reflect the views of the publisher, and the publisher hereby disclaims any responsibility for them.

ISBN: 978-1-4525-1732-2 (sc)
ISBN: 978-1-4525-1733-9 (e)

Library of Congress Control Number: 2014911277

Printed in the United States of America.

Balboa Press rev. date: 7/17/2014

For Jim.

My whole world makes sense because of you.

INTRODUCTION

It was one of my mentors, Nancy Fox, who first introduced me to the phenomenon of Spirit photography. She would show me photo after photo that she had taken while doing house clearings. I was captivated by the orbs of light and other energies not visible to the naked eye, yet clearly captured by the camera. I consider myself a fairly down-to-earth person with a reasonable dose of skepticism, so it's my nature to never embrace something just because it is true for someone else. I reserve judgment or opinion until I discover a truth for myself. In this case, God was preparing me for something, but I was completely unaware at the time.

Around this time, I had outgrown the home office that I had been using for a number of years for energy healing sessions and medium readings. At the back of our property sat a garden shed that looked similar to our house with matching siding, roof and windows. I had always dreamed of living in an English cottage, so it seemed only natural to dismantle the garden shed and build a cottage in its place. While under construction, we referred to it as "The Cottage" simply as a place holder until its real name was chosen. By the time construction was finished and the inside furnished, it was clear we needed no other name.

The plan for The Cottage always included the grounds. I wanted people to feel at peace when they came. The idea was to create a place where they could take a deep breath, let it out, and know that they were safe. So, different sections of the grounds were lovingly planted and tended. The sturdy willow oaks in the front, the gentle pines in the back, and the maples, dogwoods, and spruces in between are continually respected and valued for the wisdom they hold and freely give when asked. The walkway that brings people to The Cottage and the path that I take each day from the house are also lovingly tended and honored as they are outward expressions of our spiritual journey.

My days are spent in The Cottage joyfully holding open the delicate space between the physical and spiritual realms. This enables me to bring messages of love, understanding, and healing across the divide with gentleness and ease. When the entire house is at rest for the evening, I'd sometimes get this excited feeling in my stomach, like waking up as a kid and realizing it's my birthday, my special day. There would be a crispness - an aliveness - to the air. On those nights, I'd grab my camera, head outside to the garden, and spend hours taking pictures. If I was 'prompted' to go outside, I was never disappointed in what my camera captured.

These promptings continued from June 2010 to December 2012. During that time, I captured one stunning image after another. I never saw the energies with my physical eyes. I just followed my intuition. It never occurred to me to share them in book form until the summer of 2013 when, standing in the middle of the garden, I asked out loud, "Where is everyone?" I had enjoyed almost three years of capturing evidence that I was surrounded by light and love, even in, especially in, the darkness. The past six months of barely seeing a small orb felt as though someone had flipped a switch and it was over. The answer came immediately.

"My dear, you haven't done anything with the ones we've given you."

I sheepishly replied, "I didn't know I was supposed to."

I couldn't ignore such a clear message. The first thing I did was select the most striking images, the ones I would return to over and over to look at and wonder about. I knew I had been gifted with something quite unique, but I had no frame of reference for them.

One evening, I had them spread out on my dining room table with "Light in the Night" printed in big letters on a sheet of paper. I was looking at them in totality for the first time when a gentle, soft, almost aching, sensation started at the center of my chest and spread outward in all directions. It felt as if my heart center was opening wider than ever before, and in the next moment, I knew. The knowing was so clear that I wondered why it hadn't occurred to me before. I was looking at actual pictures of my own light in the night. They were my own council of spiritual beings and helpers, many of which had been with me since childhood, some even longer.

There was a picture of the Master Guide that was with me during the near-death experience I had as a child. There was the compassionate Teacher who came when I most needed a mother's love. I was looking at real images of Joy Guides who want only to engage the child in me to laugh and play. It was only because I had taken the pictures myself, that no part of me could deny or scrutinize what I was seeing. I was utterly blown away and spent the next few months opening wide and wider still to receive the gift I had been given. I was just beginning to feel that this was all a little too personal to share with a wider audience, when the second awareness came. This group of beloved helpers did not come to me, but through me on their way to you. They came to shine light in all those hidden-away places that keep us shut down and shut off from the love that continually surrounds us. They come as timeless doorways encouraging us to experience the light within. In the words of Neale Donald Walsh, "I have sent you nothing but angels."[1]

Spiritual Council Members

Mediums who live with a high degree of love and integrity share a common belief that the significant life events we experience are meant to awaken and expand our capacity for love. It could be love of self, others, the planet, animals, or love despite adversity, loss, or betrayal. It is also believed that we are not left alone in this journey. There are angels, spirit guides, and other light beings present on both sides of the veil to help us on our life's path and with our soul's purpose. It's easy to recognize guides on this side. Perhaps a teacher in school, mentor at work, or a cherished friend that appeared just when we needed them. However, there is also a group or council available to each of us from the spiritual plane. For when the journey has to do with love, the entire Universe conspires to help.

One day, my dear friend and spiritual advisor, Barbara Wilson, shared a perspective of the human self and the soul that spoke to me on a deep level. In essence, she explained it as follows.

Your parents made a human being, *You*, and as you were forming in your mother's womb your human story was anchoring in. For instance, you come from a long line of strong Irish people on your mother's side and hardworking people on your father's side. Your individual personality and ego were also forming as well as your physical attributes: hair and eye color, body size, and so on. There never has been, and never will be, another human being like you. As amazing as this is, that you were conceived and developed inside your mother, it's only half of the story. At the same time, a Soul or spark of divine energy began its journey from Absolute Oneness to you and your mother. Once it arrives, it lends its exquisite energy to assist in your development while it assesses the human story that is settling in with you. It wants to know if you will give it the best opportunity (through assets and challenges) to grow and expand, to polish up, if you will, a facet of its light. Its had many lifetimes before this one and knows it will have many after. In between lifetimes, it basks in the light and love of Creator for as long as it chooses so it doesn't mind in the least the challenges before it. In fact, it looks forward to them because it understands that they're only temporary and it's when it will grow the most. (In fact, it's said that a soul wants to have *every* human experience possible to achieve compassion for all of humanity. This certainly seems plausible, as we tend to have tremendous compassion for those going through a situation, if we have experienced it ourselves.)

While the Soul is assessing you and the story that is anchoring-in with you, the human you, with your personality and ego already forming, is also assessing the Soul as it wonders: "Is this the life force energy, the spark of the divine, which I want to have in *me?*"

When a "yes" is given on both sides, a soul contract is entered into and the pregnancy is carried to full term. Your beautiful God energy begins to integrate with your physical body at about the time your mother goes into labor. You are born and your lifetime begins to unfold with innumerable experiences of joy, laughter, closeness, separation, success, failure, loss, wisdom gathering, decision making. This was the essence of my friend's explanation.[2]

To view life from this perspective requires that we let go of blaming others for our life. That we stop blaming God, our parents, partners, church, government, employers, and take personal responsibility. This is not to put the blame on ourselves but to ask the next courageous question: If my soul chose these experiences from the place of unconditional love, then what quality is it yearning to bring forward? As a multifaceted diamond, you already shine in a multitude of ways. Yet there are one or two facets that you are wanting, right here, right now, to polish, and these facets are easy to find. Think of the issues you are currently dealing with. Perhaps you lost a loved one or job or you're going through a health crisis. Maybe you feel like you failed one of your children or are unable to let go of your past. Now think about the most challenging thing for you to do in light of that situation. Can you be kind and gentle with yourself? Can you set healthy boundaries or find and speak your authentic truth? Perhaps forgive yourself or someone else or choose love again even though you've suffered a tremendous hurt. These are just a few examples to get you thinking in a new direction.

From this perspective, it's easy to understand that no one is left alone on their journey. We have a whole council helping us to decide which facet of our light we want to polish, and that help continues once we arrive. The spiritual help assigned to each of us includes spirit guides, angels, healers, teachers and other specialists depending on our chosen work. These light-beings have the utmost respect and reverence for our journey and *never* interfere with or judge the choices we make. However, when invited to do so, they will step forward from behind the veil to offer loving guidance, direction, and often profound insight.

My own council members were present during times of great childhood difficulties and then reemerged in adulthood twenty-five years ago. They have *always* been with me, it's just that now I enjoy a 'front and center' relationship with them as they guide me through my work in The Cottage and in other areas of my life. They assist me in bringing through a client's loved-ones in spirit and their council members. Together they help us broaden our view of life, always through the lens of love.

Consider for a moment the message that came through for a young woman. Towards the end of the reading the woman's paternal grandmother came through asking to please get a message to her son (the client's father). Once I provided a detailed description of the grandmother, I continued with the reason she had come. The grandmother said that while she was living, she made her son feel like nothing he did was ever good enough, that no matter how hard he tried, he could never make her happy. As I shared this information with my client she was nodding her head in agreement, that her father often felt exactly as described. The grandmother continued saying that when she passed, there were literally hundreds of beautiful gifts waiting for her. When she asked what they were, she was told that they were all from her son. They were every kind thing he had ever done for her that she had rejected or dismissed. In time, she opened and received each gift her son had lovingly given her and wanted to come back and tell him a thousand thank yous. She wanted to say that it was her own closed heart that caused her to reject his love and would he please forgive her. This was such a powerful message that afterwards, with the family's permission, I shared it with a wider audience and received replies such as, "I need to call my son/daughter right now." This is precisely why mediums exist.

It's a commonly accepted phrase to say that mediums "talk to the dead." What we really do is communicate with the soul or spirit of a person that is eternal yet still holds a bit of the human ego and personality of a lifetime they've shared with you. Together, with our spiritual council, they teach us about what is truly important in life.

I invite you to view all the images in this book with your heart and not your head. The head doesn't know quite what to do with them. Besides, your heart, well, the view from your heart is heavenly.

Joy Guides

It was the Lunar Eclipse of June 2010, and I had just returned home from a wonderful evening of meditation at a friend's house. Although it was late, I wasn't ready for the night to end, so I went out into the garden to enjoy the magic of a summer's night.

I sat quietly for a bit when I noticed out of the corner of my eye a stunning being of shimmering emerald green. She was tall, pencil thin and seemed to emit from within the most splendid shades of green imaginable. I intuitively saw, felt, and heard her all at once as she pointed toward a mosquito tank nearby and said, 'Turn that off. It's hurting us." There was no judgment in her voice nor did the words denote a command. It was more of a statement, and once she delivered it she was gone. I felt a twinge of guilt; I didn't want the unit to begin with but the mosquitoes were horrid that summer making it almost unbearable to be outside in the evenings. I thought about her request. My husband had assembled the unit and it ran on propane. I wasn't keen on fooling with it in the dark, but how could I ignore this luminous being's request? I went in the house, returned with a flashlight and the instruction booklet, and after a few minutes had the unit shut down.

I sat for a while longer when an excited sensation started to build in my stomach area. I stood up, took my camera out of my pocket and started snapping pictures of each section of the yard in a panoramic fashion. Afterwards, I looked at one of the images on the camera's display screen. For a moment, I felt as if time stood still. My jaw dropped. My mind froze not knowing how to interpret what my eyes were seeing. In the next instant, I tore into the house, woke my husband from a sound sleep, put his glasses on his face, and said, "You MUST look at this." His initial irritation turned into a sheepish grin as he said, almost to himself, "That can't be anything else other than a fairy!" My once skeptical husband became a believer in that one precious moment.

The next morning I was out in The Cottage when I saw the same jubilant being come flying in and land on the edge of the coffee table. She was talking up a storm, but all I could hear was this high pitched squeaky sound that resembled air escaping from a balloon. I leaned forward and said out loud, 'I can't understand a word you're saying." With that, she flew up and landed just on the inside of my left ear. She put one hand on the top of my ear and the other hand on the bottom and made as if she was pulling my ear wide open while yelling directly into it, "Can you understand this?" I burst out laughing and couldn't stop for the longest time.

I discovered later that she was actually a Joy Guide. I had never heard of Joy Guides before; this was not surprising, since I have been accused of taking life too seriously on more than one occasion. I had to grow up fast so I guess I lost some of my carefree spirit. I was delighted to have this lighthearted being come to my rescue. Internationally, best-selling author, Sonia Choquette, says this about Joy Guides:

Your joy guides are especially fun. These are childlike essences whose purpose is to make you laugh, to invite you to play, and to encourage you to express yourself without self-consciousness. They twinkle past you all the time, trying to engage the kid in you.[3]

My sister Bonnie personifies the essence of Joy Guides. Every time we get together, we laugh so hard my sides hurt. She must have a whole horde of them in her Council. I thank God for people like her who remind us serious ones to play more. If you're like my sister, and can find humor even in the darkest of days, know that you are celebrated daily for the difference you make in the world. If you're like me, and need someone to yell in your ear occasionally, then call upon your Joy Guides to lighten things up for you.

More Cottage Joy Guides

Gnomes

In the garden is a small patch of ground cover called *Houttuynia cordata* or "Chameleon." Its variegated foliage is yellow, green and red that explodes with tiny white flowers in late summer. I had trimmed it back the previous day for the first time since planting it a few years ago. The following morning, I was enjoying a cup of coffee on the back porch when I heard a distinct, "He, He, He." It reminded me of the sound the Munchkins made when Dorothy first landed in Oz. It seemed to be coming from the ground cover, but I wasn't sure. Looking down at it I said more to myself than anyone else, "You've got to be kidding me." With a slight shake of my head to clear the early morning cobwebs, I went back to enjoying my hazelnut coffee. A moment or two later I heard it again, "He, He, He."

This time I sat straight up and with my index finger pointing upward said, "Hold on. I'll be right back." I went into the house, came back out a few moments later with the camera, and started snapping away at the ground cover. I must have taken six or seven pictures when I heard,

"You're doing it wrong!" I lowered the camera and in a slow, drawn out voice said, "Reeaallyy? Do tell."

"Put the camera up to your throat and snap from there," he said with a tone that implied my need to do this was crystal clear to everyone except me. I did as instructed and the very next picture I captured showed two small gnomes. Maybe sixteenth century folklore is true. That gnomes are small, misshapen dwarfs that guard the earth's treasures. If so, I am profoundly grateful to them for guarding the treasures of The Cottage and for teaching me the 'correct way' to take their picture.

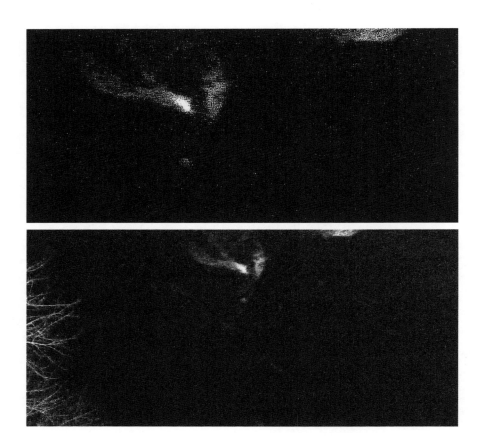

The Lighted One

Music is one of the many languages of Spirit. Have you ever awakened and heard a song playing in your head or had a song come to you out of the blue? It's usually just a snippet, part of the lyrics along with the melody. When this happens, I always pay attention.

Songs came to me one after the other, so frequently that I began to look up the lyrics and print them out. Each one contained a message that left me with more questions than answers. Instead of pushing for the answers, I decided to breathe into the space and wait. The collection of printed lyrics was piling up on the corner of my desk and one day I decided to pour over them as a whole. There was a definite pattern, or theme, that emerged that can only be described as wooing. Someone was singing love songs to me such as:

Once beneath the stars, the universe was ours, love was all I knew and all I knew was you.[4]

Close your eyes, give me your hand, darling. Do you feel my heart beating? Am I only dreaming? Or is this burning an eternal flame?[5]

So lift your eyes, if you feel you can. Reach for a star and I'll show you a plan.[6]

And say a little prayer for I, you know that if we are to stay alive, then see the peace in every eye.[7]

I'm so glad I found you, I'm not gonna lose you, whatever it takes to stay here with you, take you to the good times, see it through the bad times.[8]

I knew there was more to be discovered about this admirer and so I waited some more. The songs kept coming and soon it was Christmas of 2010 and my answer was near. Barbara had written to a group of us and suggested that we go outside Christmas night, stand under the stars and receive a Christmas blessing from Spirit. Since I have a particular affinity with the night sky, I couldn't wait to experience such a unique blessing. By this time, I never went into the garden without my camera. The temperature was well below freezing that night so it was a quick blessing and a single picture taken at the top of the pine trees along the southwest corner of the property.

I hurried back inside, shook off the cold that had gathered around me, and uploaded the image onto my computer screen. It took me a long time to understand and connect with this being's true identity. At first I thought she was an angel, then an Egyptian goddess because of the band on her forehead. It wasn't until I let go of what I thought or wanted her to be and created the space for her to draw closer that I realized she felt intensely familiar. Like a friend whose connection to me is so deep we transcend all other human relationships. A friend who holds the knowledge of every detail about me without a speck of judgment giving me the sudden urge to be more than I've ever been before.

This experience made me realize that some people shine their light as brightly as they can right from the start of their lives and keep shining it until they take their last breath. Others keep their light as far away as possible. Their life's work then becomes calling it forward little by little until one day it shows up in all its glory and says, "I am Here, Now, I am Love, I AM You."

When I fully and completely embraced my Lighted One, all of my relationships began to change. For if I'm accepted without judgment, then so are you. If I am full and alive and open with possibilities, then you must be too. When we expand in this way, we fall in love with every person we meet.

Kuan Yin

A full year had passed since taking the Lighted One's picture. When the family gatherings of Christmas Day were over, Jim and I put our feet up to relax a bit. We wanted to watch a new DVD called: *Orbs: The Veil is Lifting* with Klaus Heinemann, Ph.D.[9] It's the first full-length film that brings together scientists, spiritual teachers, and experts to explore the orb phenomenon. It shows viewers how to take successful orb photographs with a simple digital camera. What fascinated me the most about the information they presented was their discussion of a phenomenon called mist or plasma photography. It's where orbs or the energy of orbs congeal together into amazing shapes and designs. It was exhilarating to watch as they showed photo after photo of this type of photography while experts from different fields discussed how and why the camera lens captures energy not otherwise seen by the naked eye. It also explained the photo of the Lighted One. With my heart bursting and my mind expanding with new information, I couldn't wait to go outside and snap away.

Back inside, I uploaded the pictures onto my laptop. One image stood out among the group. It contains the energy and expression of the beautiful Kuan Yin, the best-loved deity in the Chinese world. While almost unknown to the Western world, Kuan Yin is the mystery and power of the Divine Feminine. She transcends all doctrines, creeds, and traditions.[10] She brings the vibration of great compassion and is devoted to helping us fully open up to our spiritual gifts, attain profound knowledge and enlightenment, and reduce world suffering.

She is depicted throughout the centuries as either standing on a lotus flower or riding a dragon. Her powerful energy came to me that Christmas night of 2011 riding a dragon when the Chinese calendar was just about to shift from the Year of the Rabbit into the Year of the Dragon. Her graceful hands are usually shown in one of three possible ways, one of which is holding a branch of vegetation. While it's unclear exactly what she is holding in this picture, her graceful hand by the branch of my maple tree is undeniable.

Once I understood the picture, I was eager to find out why she revealed herself to me in such a realistic way. I remember going into meditation thinking, "I'm ready, let's do this, let's connect, let's embrace." Time after time, I showed up to the meditation chair and... nothing. Since the beginning of my spiritual journey, a connection with God as Father came easily. However, connecting with the divine feminine was proving to be quite a challenge. As time went by I realized it was inextricably connected to my relationship with my own mother who passed in 1999. I had long since forgiven her for being a mother who did not like to touch or be touched, something all children need. I began to wonder if on an unconscious level I was keeping myself at arm's length from Kuan Yin.

One day I was sitting in the living room looking at an 18" cast iron statue of Kuan Yin when the urge came over me to pick it up and examine it. I leaned back into my chair and put the statute on a cushion in my lap. Almost immediately I became mesmerized as the child within me began touching, exploring, drinking in every inch of the statue as if it was Kuan Yin herself. The Goddess seemed to be totally accepting of this tactical expression of love from a purely innocent part of me. While my mind said, "It's only a statue," it was a starting place, a safe place for the child part of me to test the waters. I felt vulnerable and uncomfortable letting this small part of me come forward. She was so used to having her hands slapped away. However, this time she found only an invitation to explore more.

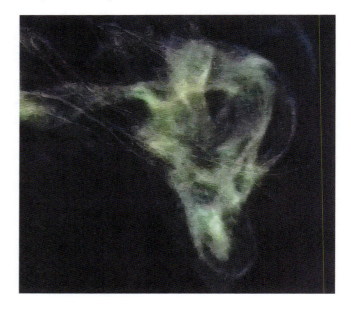

Perhaps it's the childlike parts of us that allow or block our connection to Spirit by projecting our experiences of mom and dad onto Mother/Father God. This can be a positive projection allowing us to fully open and connect with a power greater than ourselves. Or, if our upbringing was a challenging one, then those same parts may expect similar treatment from a bigger, more powerful Parent God.

The next morning's meditation felt like a soft breeze that lifted and carried me through a window that had opened the day before. At once, I found myself in a peace-filled Zen garden where I saw a young version of myself sitting on her heels in the warm grass sharing tea with Kuan Yin. I floated effortlessly into this version of me and drank in the beauty of the Goddess that I knelt before. My heart repeated Teacher, Teacher, Teacher, with utter devotion and respect. For me, speaking and feeling the word Teacher meant that Kuan Yin was someone I trusted with every cell of my being. This was significant since I grew up having to rely mostly on my own resources. Hearing myself say Teacher began the process of melting away years of self-sufficiency and self-reliance.

As the meditation continued, it had the look and feel of being centuries ago. I had left my home to live on the temple grounds. We sat there, she on slightly higher ground than I, as immense love flowed from me to her and back again. It looked like tiny flowers of different varieties and colors and fragrance swaying like a hammock between us. In that moment, there was no one else in the world but she and I.

I came out of the meditation with a solidness, a fullness at my core that remains to this day. I pray that your own mother reflects for you the constant and abiding love of the Divine Feminine. If she could not be this mirror for you or, if she was and is now in Spirit, know this one thing is true: God as Mother is eternally yours for you belonged to her heart long before your earthly mother bore you in this lifetime. She will do everything in her power to bridge the divide and share a cup of tea with you. She understood my difficulty in connecting with her better than I did. Her energy will always be connected to her picture in case you need her, too. I wholeheartedly encourage you to go and sit for a while. Let the layers of separation fall away. Go, no matter how long the journey takes. She will undoubtedly hold up the mirror of truth and fill your heart with the sweet aroma of love. In that moment, you will know that she has loved you for always and then she will say, "Come, let me teach you again."

Additional Mist Photos

Woman In Lower Right Hand Corner

Animal Totem: White Stallion

Orbs

With the introduction of digital photography in 1988, cameras now have the potential to capture higher frequencies in a way that film cameras rarely did. To understand the orb phenomenon, it is important to remember that everything in our Universe is energy. Science, through Quantum Physics, is finding that even things that appear solid (like my wooden end table) is not matter at all but, at the sub-atomic level, pure energy vibrating at a particular frequency.[11] Some frequencies are in the range of sound and some in the range of color. Award-winning composer and sound healer, Steven Halpern, PhD, says that:

"Vibrations at 1000 cycles per second are easily audible. If you double the vibrations to 2000 cycles per second, that is one octave higher. If you double it again to 4000 cycles per second, that is another octave. A normal piano spans a bit more than seven octaves. If, hypothetically, we could extend the piano keyboard another 35 to 50 octaves higher, the keys at the higher end would produce colors, rather than audible sounds, when played."[12]

Each person also has their own vibration. The more we meditate, the more we focus on love and joy and bliss, our individual vibrations (the range of notes we are playing on our own piano) move up the frequency scale. The higher up the scale we go the more access we have to higher planes of consciousness where joy, happiness, and inspiration live.

I have hundreds of photographs of orbs in all shapes, sizes and colors. I have studied, interacted, and meditated with them and have come to my own conclusions about these fascinating balls of light. For instance, I believe that many orbs captured in photos are actually our own emanated energy. We live in a sea of thoughts, in a sea of consciousness. Yours, mine, and ours. The world we live in today is a result of our planet's collective thoughts, attitudes, beliefs, emotions and so on. We are constantly releasing energy into our world.

I once spoke at a women's unity retreat. After dinner, a powerful conversation took place among the women seated at my table. After witnessing their courageous truth-telling, I spontaneously turned to the woman next to me and shared something I had never shared openly before. Later that night, I returned home feeling renewed and wanted the garden to bear witness to my experience. I sat under the maple tree with the camera held up to my throat and repeated aloud, "I told," while taking pictures. This is what truth telling looks like energetically. I like to think that the energy I sent out into the world that night is encouraging someone else to speak their own truth.

There are other orbs that appear to be in a class all their own. Their centers contain intricate detail, their colors vibrant. They have a condensed nucleus and appear to radiate from within. I believe some of these energies are higher dimensional beings. Most of the energies captured in photos contained in this book travelled to The Cottage garden as something, most likely condensed energy orbs. Think of it this way. Any time we receive an inspirational thought out of the blue or find ourselves in an awful mood and spontaneously shift out of it, that's energy and it travelled to you as something. Quite possibly, it came from one of your council members as an orb that inspired or changed you in a positive way.

Orbs can also be loved ones in spirit, family members who have left their physical bodies and, as souls, are now travelling at the speed of thought. Souls continue to grow and evolve once they drop the denseness of their physical bodies. When the walls we constructed while alive slowly dissolve, only love remains. It's love that is at the core of our connections with the living and the deceased. Orbs of our loved ones in spirit are often seen in pictures right alongside of our own emanated energy, especially at joyous events such as weddings, graduations, births, and special family gatherings.

After sharing some of my orb photos with my older sister, Linda, she tried her hand at taking her own orb pictures, but was unsuccessful, so she lost interest. A few months later, she took a trip to visit family on the West Coast and was standing on the balcony of her hotel room one evening taking in the gorgeous scenery. The whole courtyard was filled with people talking, dining, groups here and there bursting out in laughter. She said the entire scene was magical. As she took out her camera she began talking to the energy of the evening saying, "I know you're here and I feel a connection to you. If you would like to make yourself known on my camera, know that I am open with gratitude for this moment." In saying this prayer, Linda had aligned herself with the energy of the evening. Afterwards, she uploaded two photos for me to see. Both contained no less than a hundred orbs. They were everywhere and contained both higher dimensional beings in stunning colors as well as sparkling orbs emanating from all present, including my sister.

People often ask my opinion about the orbs in their own photos. I don't mind sharing what I see but I encourage them to sit with the photo and trust what comes to them. While I've shared with you examples of our own energy as well as other worldly orbs, there are many images that appear to be orbs but are only the result of condensation on the camera lens or in the air. These orbs appear flat, one dimensional, with little or no definition to them. Also, all other objects in the photo appear behind the orbs. So view your own orb photos with scrutiny and consider what was going on with you and around you when the picture was taken. If it is "in a class all its own," know that the orb chose to let their energy be captured for a reason, and it's up to you to discover why. It just may hold information that helps you expand your view of yourself and life.

While deciding which orb photos to include in the book, I would often get lost in the wonderment of them and the beautiful energy they still exude. I was particularly captivated by several images I had of the same blue orb, always by itself. While connecting with it, I gently heard the term "witness." The witness is the thoughtless observer within us, or a state of being in consciousness that is purely witnessing life take place without contemplating differences. It is a state of complete acceptance without personal bias to alter the event, find fault, take credit or judge.[13] It is also a state that can be achieved through daily meditation where we witness our thoughts going by without reacting to them. I began to consider if I was reacting to situations in my life, taking them a little too personally, instead of watching them peacefully pass by. This coincided with what Kuan Yin was teaching me about staying centered regardless of what life brings our way.

Master Guide

Everyone has one preeminent guide in their council called the Master Guide. While other guides come and go depending on where we are on our life's path, the Master Guide's presence remains constant. Personal stories abound of people lifted to safety in the midst of great tragedy. Our Master Guide oversees our safety as well as our life's plan. They always lift us to safety whether we survive the trauma or are carried gently home. I have brought through scores of loved ones who have passed tragically. While the evidence that comes through for each reading is unique, one constant truth prevails. They felt no pain. Their spirits left their body a split second before the event occurred. This truth was echoed in my own experience.

I mentioned earlier that my childhood was challenging. It was also dysfunctional and, at times, intensely abusive. My Master Guide was always there on those really bad nights holding my 'essence' safe and away from what was happening to my physical body. He strengthened and sustained me. Once, when I was 9 years old, I was rushed to Sinai Hospital in Baltimore. I saw everything from the ceiling as they wheeled me down the hall and into a room, the nurse shouting, "We're losing her!" Next, I was aware of standing beside the bed looking at myself lying there. My Master Guide was next to me holding my hand. He asked if I would like to go for a walk. My whole being answered "yes." As we turned and walked away, I felt myself get smaller and smaller until I went right into his heart. I never wanted to leave. The next thing I knew I ached from head to toe. I was back in my body.

In my early thirties I started seeing a therapist who was skilled in healing post traumatic stress. At the same time, I began exploring spiritual concepts such as the idea that we choose our parents. I had a difficult time with that one because I thought it meant that I deserved what had happened to me. One day, while on my lunch hour, I was sitting in my car journaling. I had had a particularly difficult therapy session the day before that left me just angry enough to ask, "If I chose my parents, and I mean IF, then I want to talk to the part of me that did."

I immediately heard an innocent voice say, "I did."

"Please tell me what the &*%# you were thinking." The reply took me off guard. I heard: "We had spent many lifetimes basking in the light while the soul known as our father had spent many lifetimes caught in the darkness. It was only right that we come out of the light to help him get out of the darkness."

I was blown away. I sat quietly for a bit trying to take in this new perspective when it dawned on me that I must have failed. My father died suddenly one day in 1979. It was too late. I didn't do what I set out to do. Again,

I heard the soft voice. "You didn't fail. First you had to experience his darkness and survive it. Then remember it. (I had blocked the worst of it out.) Then make a decision to heal. It's in the healing that you bring light into your own darkness. As you do this, you also bring light into your father's darkness."

In that moment, I couldn't do anything but own my truth and say, "He wasn't worth it." It was a statement not a question, however, the reply still came. "How do you think he got caught in the darkness to begin with? He came out of the light to help someone else get out of their darkness."

The next time I saw my Master Guide was early June 1998. I was still working full time and had taken a week off to celebrate turning 40. He walked right into my bedroom one night as I was praying. My mediumship gifts were just beginning to return although I didn't understand it at the time. We sat and talked and cried and talked and cried. It felt so natural. I remember telling my husband that I was having some sort of spiritual awakening. He said it sounded more like church. We both laughed. The visits continued for about three weeks. I wanted them to last forever but the very nature of life is ever evolving and changing. One evening he said that it was the last time. I was about to say, "Wait! What do you mean the last time," but he was already getting smaller and smaller. Then, as a bright point of light, he moved right into my heart center. All I could do was softly whisper his name, "Jesus."

I continued on my healing journey for as long as it took, no matter how difficult it was. I refused to give up. I continued until I could shine my own light, clear and bright in each of those ugly experiences. Until I could feel nothing but compassion and love for myself and those involved. Some days were easier than others. In the end, I realized that underneath it all, I love my dad. I love my mom. That was huge for me. Then I realized that if underneath all of my hurt and pain there was nothing but love for them, then underneath all of their hurt and pain, there had to be nothing but love for me and my sisters.

Your own Master Guide protects you just as beautifully. He or she is constrained only by our free-will choices and our soul's mission. However, within those boundaries, they joyfully move heaven and earth for us.

Spiritual Healing And The Helpers

I was first introduced to Harry Edwards in June 2012 by Rev. Hoyt Robinette, a brilliant physical medium. Rev. Hoyt asked if I was familiar with the work of Harry Edwards. When I shook my head no, he said, "Well, he's here in Spirit and he definitely knows you and your work at The Cottage. I suggest you read up on him." I was skeptical yet curiously excited since this was the first time I was aware of a guide working with me that had had a physical lifetime. When I returned home, it took no time at all to discover that Mr. Edwards was born in London in 1893 and opened his own healing sanctuary in Surrey, England in 1935. Because of his work in the field of spiritual healing, he became world-renowned with his center still in operation today. I ordered many of the books he had written along with a guided meditation recorded in his own voice.

While some spirit guides live as energy, in the cosmic realm, or as very high level light beings, some are also persons who have lived many former lifetimes and advanced beyond a need to reincarnate. In his book, *A Guide for the Development of Mediumship*, Mr. Edwards explains that, "A guide's mission is to help and guide us in our earthly existence. They are noble personalities of good intent and are attracted to humans where there exists a common bond."[14] For example, a guide who takes much pleasure in music, art, science, or healing, will seek to attend someone who has an inherent similarity or latent gifts. Since meeting Mr. Edwards that spring, I have made important shifts around using my gifts in a more cohesive manner, combining prayer, attunement to Spirit, and the vibration of pure love.

Spiritual healing is based on the belief that all change comes from within; that our outer world is but an outward expression of our inner world. When we go deep within, we connect with ourselves on a spiritual level, a soul level where everything exists in beautiful harmony and balance. Even our struggles and challenges have meaning, purpose. We learn to step away from the human story that we all carry to ask the next empowered question: What quality is my spirit longing to bring forward in this particular situation? We pray for the grace and the willingness to live in the answer. Spiritual healing can create deep shifts in our lives whether we are longing to live more courageously or are preparing to let go and journey home. I love what Elizabeth Cosmos, PhD., says in her book *Ama-Deus: Healing with Sacred Energy of the Universe*, "When one chooses the path to heal, an opportunity opens to reevaluate the meaning of life. To heal is to bring into sharper focus the situation creating distress; not as a hopeless victim but rather as an empowered participant."[15]

With the help of my Master Guide, Harry Edwards and many gifted teachers on this side, my healing work in The Cottage continued to deepen and expand. Another Christmas was approaching and my three year journey of capturing spirit photography was coming a close. This last photo was taken on December 25, 2012. When I realized it was strikingly similar to a photo in Harry Edward's *Spirit Healing* book, I immediately wrote to his sanctuary in Surrey and received permission to publish his picture alongside mine.[16] In it, Harry Edwards, on the left, is offering healing to a young girl with his colleague and dear friend, Ray Branch, assisting. They worked together like this, one in front of and the other behind the person seeking healing, for the better part of twenty years. I have often wondered if it was Mr. Edwards' knowledge of physical mediumship in concert with my own gifts that manifested the images in this book. If so, it is fitting to close with his picture and my profound gratitude.

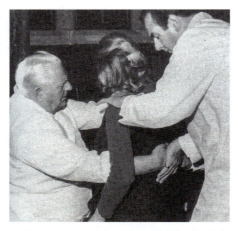

In Closing

All of the Light Beings in this book broke through the veil of separation to sing a love song just for you. Whether you connect with the Lighted One, Master Guide, Joy Guides or others, they all came through me on their way to you. They are external expressions of the wonderment of spirit that is within and among us always. If we view the Spirit realm through the lens of Hollywood movies, ghost hunting shows, vampires and the like, then our connection 'home' will be cloaked with an element of fear. However, if we view the Spirit realm as the indigenous indians do with soul songs, dance and great joy, then all that we capture will truly be our light in the night.

Until Only Love Remains

In Gratitude

Writing this book has profoundly changed my life. It started with hearing, "You haven't done anything with the ones (pictures) we've given you," and a willingness to share them with a wider audience. Little did I know that the energy of each photo was still present and had so much to teach me. I am profoundly grateful to Spirit's unending patience and persistence with me as without both this book would not have made it into print.

The process of writing this book and remaining present for all that The Cottage offers to others, required an exorbitant amount of support from my husband, Jim. His unwavering belief in my abilities along with his unconditional love and support is a gift to me each and every day.

Editors are rare and treasured gifts. Love and gratitude to Rose Michaels and Emily Cain for your expertise and patience with my unique writing process. To Tina Evans for your encouraging words and helpful suggestions. To Nick Proudfoot of ProudDesigns.net for your stunning expertise in getting the photos ready for print.

When you step into a brand new arena, you need someone to take hold of your hand and not let go until you're finished. My un-biological sister, Beth Leitner, was a constant source of insight and guidance on this project. Beth helped me find the courage to delve deeper and share more. She is an extraordinary gift in my life as well as a talented artist and illustrator.

To my sisters Bonnie and Linda. What an unusual journey we share. The three of us coming full circle over the past year fills my heart in ways I have no words to describe. To my grandson, Jayden, a bright light in my life and one of the reasons my heart sings. Thank you for always asking me, "How you comin' on your book, Nana?"

Gratitude to all who have come to The Cottage over the years. Whether you came once or often, you helped to make it into the magical place it is today. Many of you were attending classes over the three year period and saw the photos and heard my experiences first hand. You came with me into that sacred space of waiting to discover all that these light beings wanted to share. Thank you for being such great company.

Honor and respect to Elizabeth Cosmos, Nancy Fox, Christine Garwood, Nancy Michaelson, Ellen Potter, and Barbara Wilson. Thank you for lighting the way for so many of us.

REFERENCES

1 Walsh, Neale Donald, Conversations with God - Book 2, 2005, Hampton Roads Publishing and The Penguin Group, New York, New York, p. 343.

2 Wilson, Barbara, Psychology Professor at Towson State College, Towson, Maryland. Conversation on 6/6/2008 at Nancy Fox's.

3 Choquette, Sonia, Ask Your Guides, 2006, Hay House, page 161.

4 Moody Blues, Your Wildest Dreams, The Other Side of Life. Universal Motown Records Group, 1989. CD.

5 The Bangles, Eternal Flame, Everything: Best of the Bangles. Columbia Europe, 2001. CD.

6 Air Supply. Lost in Love, Lost in Love. Arista, 1990. CD.

7 Cole, Paula. I Don't Want to Wait, This Fire. Warner Brothers, 1996. CD.

8 The Starting Line, Nothing's Gonna Stop Us Now, With Hopes of Starting Over. Drive Thru Records, 2001. CD.

9 Klaus Heinimann, Ph.D., Orbs: The Veil is Lifting, DVD

10 Palmer, Martin; Ramsay, Jay; Man-Ho Kwok, The Kuan-Yin Chronicles, Hampton Roads Publishing, Charlottesville, VA 2009, Back cover

11 One Mind One Energy website www.one-mind-one-energy.com/Law-of-vibration.html

12 Halpern, Steven, Sound Health – The Music and Sound That Make Us Whole, Harper & Row, New York, New York, 1985, p. 182

13 Original author of the witness definition is unknown. Language included is widely accepted and used throughout many sources.

14 Edwards, Harry, A Guide for the Development of Mediumship, Herbert Jenkins Ltd, London, England, 1960, p.22

15 Cosmos, Elizabeth, PhD, Ama-Deus: Healing with the Sacred Energy of the Universe, Xlibris Corp. 2012, Page 171.

16 Edwards, Harry, Spirit Healing, Herbert Jenkins Ltd., London, England, p. 49. Printed with permission from Harry Edwards Healing Sanctuary, Shere, UK, www.harryedwardshealingsanctuary.org.uk.

Made in the USA
Lexington, KY
30 October 2014